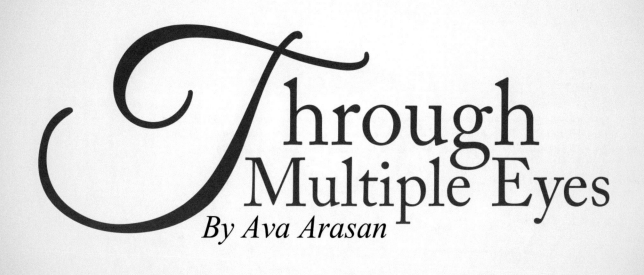

Through Multiple Eyes

By Ava Arasan

Balboa Press books may be ordered through booksellers or by contacting:

Balboa Press
A Division of Hay House
1663 Liberty Drive
Bloomington, IN 47403
www.balboapress.com
1 (877) 407-4847

Because of the dynamic nature of the Internet, any web addresses or links contained in this book may have changed since publication and may no longer be valid. The views expressed in this work are solely those of the author and do not necessarily reflect the views of the publisher, and the publisher hereby disclaims any responsibility for them.

Interior Graphics/Art Credit: Ava Arasan

ISBN: 978-1-9822-0824-0 (sc)
ISBN: 978-1-9822-0825-7 (e)

Library of Congress Control Number: 2018908514

Print information available on the last page.

Balboa Press rev. date: 08/13/2018

BALBOA.
PRESS
A DIVISION OF HAY HOUSE

Through Multiple Eyes

Here you shall very much enjoy
This wonderful book of poetry,
That explores many subjects,
Some new,
Some old,
Some frightening,
Some bold,
And through these various subjects,
You will see multiple parts of the world,

Through multiple dimensions,
Through multiple times,
Through multiple emotions,
Through multiple eyes.

The Topic of My Poem

I do not know what the topic of my poem is,
I do not know what the title of my poem is,
I do not know what I should write about in my poem,

Oh! I see!

The topic of my poem is
I don't know what the topic of my poem is,

Oh! I know!

The title of my poem is the "Topic of my Poem",

Oh! I understand now!

The idea that I should write about in my poem is what the topic of my poem is!

Here's my poem!

A Forest

A bush rattles,
A pond ripples,
A stick cracks,
A leaf crunches,

For a being with the heart of a city,
These noises can cause great pity,

A weed rustles,
A tree howls,
A cloud thunders,
A river bustles,

On a simple walk in the forest, these noises have been known,
To unnerve the wary listener and
scare them to their bones,

Unlike the loud honks,
Constant shouting,
And whirring of a car,

These sounds are unknown and frightening,
For you know you have heard the noises,
Yet don't know what still poises,
Beyond the cracking stick,
The rippling pond,
The falling dirt,
And the crunching leaves,

Without a sense of security,
You are left there cold and shivering to dream,
About all the creatures that are stalking you

Behind their very own protective screen,

Although you are afraid there is no reason to be,
This mysterious creature,
is safely tucked behind a tree,
And is probably still cowering there,
Because you have given it quite a scare!

Being afraid of something will never release
a sense of security and wonderful peace,

It will only leave you cold and bare,
Feeling that you only have the power to stand and stare,

Instead of worrying yourself, alone on the path,
Try to glimpse this forest wonder through a joyful eye,
And then those
Rusling weeds,
Howling trees,
Thundering clouds,
And bustling rivers,
Will no longer seem out of place,
For now you know that they are part of the forest,
Every single animal, plant, rock, and noise,

With this new recognition,
And a peaceful mission,
You may realize that you are no longer out of place too,
Because now the forest and all of its beings,
Are a part of you.

Among Puffy White Clouds

The clouds shift into any form that they please,
They may swoop to touch the ground,
Or they stay around
enjoying the sweet rays of sun,

They take entertaining forms that we enjoy
down in our own little town,

They bounce around in different colors,
A misty gray or a puffy white,
The wonderful clouds are entertaining up there,

And as the breeze tousles your hair,
You remained transfixed
You're only able to stand and stare,
And let wild pictures run through your mind
Of what gorgeous form lies behind,
The joyous, round clouds,

When the clouds start to cry
Their blue tears of laughter,
They spread their jewels,
About the land,

And I don't even to try,
To escape being swept up into flight,
Along with the puffy white clouds,
With their friendly, glowing light,

They share 'round their laughter,
And their happy stories,
They manage to make a heart feel light,
With absolutely zero plight.

When You are Different

When you are different,
Someone will sneer,
The class will jeer,
And you may shed a tear,

When you are different,
You feel all left out,
And no matter how hard you shout,
No one will care to hear,

When you are different,
You are laughed at and teased,
Quickly you are stung by thousands of bees,

When you are different,
Your mouth will snap shut,
A fellow will smile,
And toss away the key,

When you are different,
Life can be hard,
It can leave many experiences
Rotten and charred,

Yet,

When you are unique,
Pathways unfold,

You can be yourself,
Beautiful and bold,

When you are unique,
People will stand and stare,
At your marvelous being,

And you will not care,
If a nasty, scared fellow,
Walks up to your door,
All of their comments will give you a bore,

For when you are unique,
And happy with yourself,

You will write your own story,
And add it to the shelf.

A Magic Mirror

As I walk through the glistening white streets,
The cold blanket of snow calls to me,
With the way it glistens in sunlight and moonlight,
The way it crunches under my feet,
How it inspires me with ideas,
How its clear, bumpy surface serves as a mirror,

And when I look into this mirror,
I see truth and love,
Happiness and joy,
And I suddenly feel warm through the cold.
It's the simple effect of a magic mirror,
Whose wonderful stories remain untold.

Essence of Truth

My Mother said to me one day,
A day that I felt was wasted away.
She said, "Be yourself and rule your way,"

"From today and forever your
True Essence flies,
Your worries and guilt will say their goodbyes,"

"You have always possessed this essence of truth,"
"This magical power is wealthier than gold,"

"And this my darling you are to hold."

Flames

I see the fire in your eyes little girl,
I see the flames sting your arms
And the ash gray your hair,

I see your home burn
And your life turn,

But there is hope little girl,
Hope for a better life,
Hope that war will end,
Hope for a lifetime of peace,

So keep on going little girl,
Rise from the ash,
And raise your head up high,

Walk towards your freedom
And say goodbye
To the pain that had scarred your life,

Hope is your key little girl,
Hope is it all you need.

The Simple Loveliness of Books!

I'm being sucked in!
I can't pull myself out!
It is taking control of my brain!

"What is it?" you ask,

The simple loveliness of books,
That's what!

They entertain me
And sustain me
With adventure.

With my book,
I can learn about a world,
Whether real or fantasy,
What they are,
And what they aren't.

My book is a beacon of light that will show me the way
any day!

Now,

I better get back to reading!

Types of Wind

A sweet summer breeze,
A swirl of adventure,
Bringing warm cheer,
And rousing good spirits,

A cold winter chill,
A flurry of snowflakes,
Transporting warm memories,
And recovering blankets,

A long autumn wind,
A heap of dry leaves,
Kicking up fun
And shouting out laughter,

A small spring puff,
A rustle of petals,
Showing audacious colors,
And valleys of green,

These types of wind,
Enticing all memories,
Add a charm to any day,
Here or very far away,

Just simply listen to what they say!

Complete!

With a satisfied sigh,
I look away from my books,

All is now finished,
Very full, lies my pride,

Now, I can sing,
And soar up to the clouds,

Knowing no more work lies below,
For now,

With a satisfied smile,
I stare out my window,

I have nicely finished
My large pile of work,

And now I dance,
And groove to that beat,

For everything is nicer,
When all is complete.

The Melody Movers

First key, second key, third key,
I'm playing my favorite melody,

My fingers fly across the keys,
My heart sings with the tune,
My hands dance to the quickening rhythm,
My feet thump on the ground,

This is me
when I play
my beautiful and trusted
piano.

Rain Racers

The raindrops are racing down my window,
I wonder which will win,
I quietly give them names
And watch them until the moon is high in the sky,

The moon's dazzling rays flow down on the raindrops
So that when they run,
They look like the shooting stars that decorate the sky,

I watch them until I feel sleepy,
Their brilliant performance still playing in my mind,
I feel very calm and rested,
And finally,

When I do go to sleep,
I am still quite aware that
the rain racers
are still there
racing.

Painting with Puddles

I grab my brush and toss paint on my canvas,
I'm not in a rush,
I feel like I have all the time in the world,

I love to watch my colors splash,

Across my evening scene,
Across my golden sunset,
Across my puffy white sky,
Across tiny houses,
Across people's faces and
Even across me.

The Land of You

It can be a gate
depending on you,
It can be a star
depending on you,
It is whatever you choose,
but they all lead to
the world
of you,
I am part of you too
depending on you,

In your world of whatever you desire
Is simply whatever is right for you,
Whatever you feel in this land of you,
is perfectly alright for you to feel,

So be yourself in this land
for
YOU.

Question Rules?

Have a question about something?
Wanna ask it?

First, think to yourself,
Should I?
Could I?
Would I?
May I?
Can I?
If the answer is yes, then the answer is yes!
No question about it!

Brain Yoga

Stretch your brain,
Squeeze it
Roll it,
Toss it,
You have all it takes to be great in your way,
Think creatively, do not be the same,
So,
Bounce it,
Shelter it,
Stretch it,
Squeeze it,
Roll it,
Toss it,
BE IT!

Disappointment

Disappointment is like a huge rock,
A weight on one's shoulder
That drags them far down,
And really far under

Disappointment is a little bang,
That rings through one's stomach,
Tensing up and breaking down,
Causing confidence to plummet,

Do not be disappointed in yourself,
For you shall realize soon,
The only thing that disappointment does,
Is be harmful to you,

Love yourself through and through,
And whenever one does announce,
Something that will make you sad,
Do not let disappointment pounce,

Hold your head up high and say it clear,
"Nothing can bring me down from here!
For I know myself through and through,
And no disappointment will turn me blue."

Magic, Magic

Magic, magic, in the sky,
Will you teach me how to fly?
To travel beyond the terrestrial limit,
To fly higher than the highest cloud?

Magic, magic, from the sea,
Let me ride your waves and be free,
Let me swim in your deepest wonders,
Let me enjoy your gorgeous waters,

Magic, magic, from my land,
You have given me a helping hand,
To see the sky and the sea and their beauty,
Will you let me explore more?

Magic, Magic, right in me,
You are all and everything I am to be.

The Delightful Shade of Gray

The fog's moist molecules melt on my skin,
They wrap me in a warm blanket
And block out fear.

They stir my inner truth
And make me excited,
This is my delightful shade of gray.

Under a large pillow,
With the cloudiest of clouds,
I try not to let the gloomy weather,
Bring me down,

Yet instead see the best,
And do not let escape,
The glorious beginnings,
Of a record-breaking day!
So I set off to enjoy my delightful shade of gray!

Ready? Set? RUN!

Sweat drips down my face,
Every muscle in my body aches,
I radiate heat,
Just like the sun,

My eyes on my target,
My mind in my game,
My soul like a wolf,
Ready to pounce on its prey,

The wind on my back,
Tousling my brown hair,
The mud on my legs,
The grass shivering underneath my feet,

As I get ready to make my move,
I get into this groove,
To try and win the game,

I sprint across the field,
Taking full yield,
To running players on the other team,

As I rush to the safe zone,
I dodge my chasers,
Kicking up a cloud of
Soft brown dirt,

I land in my haven
And grab my prize,
Full of adrenaline,
I open my eyes,

I scan my surrounding,
And hear victorious cries,
Of others who have made it back,
With that same prize,

I prepare for my sprint,
Back to my home base,
Nervous little butterflies,
Tickle my inside and my face,

I take a deep breath,
Prepping for this run,
I know that if I make it
I'll have lots more fun,

The risk at hand
I know very well,
Having to sit in the "prison",
Does not feel swell,

With my pointers in mind,
I take my time,

And then…

RUN!

451

Which tower shall we build higher?
One of crackling electricity and widescreens
Or one with yellowed pages
And covers quite clean,

Shall we line our minds with
Glowing bright lights,
Or with words so powerful
To light up the nights,

Should we always walk the streets
With a phone in our hand or
Gaze at the delicate words
That are so very grand,

Shall we always need a picture
Painted for us
Or shall we draft our dreams
In clouds in our minds,

Shall we always roam around
two steps behind?

When we choose to sit at home
And absorb for hours,
Instead of consuming the words
And digesting them for ourselves
creating thousands of colors

And dreams we can smell,

Shall we choose the easy path
That is carved out before us,

Or shall we shape our own path,
And let ourselves guide us?

The Night at Your Core

While the night dances around the buildings,
One knows what must be done:

To take out a candle with a frown on one's face
To chase out the darkness from your private space,
To shoo away the night from its rightful place,

This really should not be the case,

To have the night and light around your mindset,

Will leave a healthy trace,

Because along with having light,
You must form your character with the night at your base.

Red Wonder

You
can never break
down my world of wonder,
My world of beautiful thunder,
You may succeed to take down what you think,
But no matter how hard you desire,
You can never demolish
My blazing red
Fire.

Christmas Magic

A little giggle escapes my mouth
as I bend over to see,
The piles of little presents,
Stacked under the Christmas tree,

I pick each up
one by one,
Quietly examining,
What on earth could be,
Inside the lovely present,
Under that tree!

I touch the ornate wrapping,
And fiddle with ribbons and bows,
And somewhat eye suspiciously,
That good ol' mistletoe,

Outside, the lights twinkle,
All wrapped outside the house,
It's so calm you could hear the footsteps,
Of a little gray mouse,

The pets are dressed with bells,
And tiny scarfs too,
While the family is piled 'round the tree,
Wondering what is next to do,

Santa hats are on top heads,
Adding to holiday cheer,
The table is piled with food,
And maybe a little bit of beer,

Smiles are pasted on faces,
And laughter is a bell,
That rings around the circle,
Causing joy to swell,

The Christmas magic bustles,
As all lay quiet to hear,
The soft thudding hoofs,
Of Santa's cute reindeer.

The clock strikes eight,
And then we all look to see,
If any more presents,
Have reached the Christmas tree,

These memories will not be forgotten,
In three years or one or two,
But will be carried in the little Christmas child,
Whose laugh rings through you.

Haven's Wing

They can flutter,
They can fly,
Way up high in any sky,
Life for them must be a piece of pie,

Ever and ever they are free,
To be and to be who they are to be,

They have the gift of black stung wings
And as they glide above the earth
their surroundings sing,

Yes, the life of a raven,
Must be a haven.

Smile Juice

"Hold still,"
"Say cheese,"

"Cheese."

Compared to a real smile

Of love,
Of joy,
Of smarts,
Of accomplishment,
Of prominence,

That was fake.

There are many different smiles

Smiles of
malice,
doom,
and darkness,

Smiles of joy,
glory,
wits,

So,
pump some smile juice in,
to make your smile worthwhile!

Sky?

Sky, dear sky, how far do you fly?
You seep into the universe,
I know that all right!
But how far, just how far
do you go?

You can travel into everlasting night,
And leave no trace of how distant you whereabouts might light.

What is beyond what I cannot see?
Why can't you show me how you are so free?

You can slip into every undiscovered corner,
And many of those there are, unseen,

One day, whenever you please,
I will follow you
into these.

The Last Bite

Take that last bite,
Race that last step,
Grab that last goal,
Swim that last lap,
Climb that last rung,

Put in that last effort.

What Defines You.

A bad mark does not define you,
Neither does a scar,
Or a terrible scrape,
Neither does a feature of your face,

Nasty comments do not define you,
Aching hearts,
Flowing tears,
Shattered eyes,
Do not define you,

Piles of makeup or,
Types of clothing
do not define you,

Your effort and your heart are what you are,
Do not let the society force you behind bars,

That will hinder the being that you are meant to be,
You are yourself and you should believe
That everything about you is perfect and cool,

So live up to your standards,
And simply do what you feel in your heart
is right for you,

Your spirit is the only thing that matters here,
Please keep love extremely near
To yourself and let it flow and flow,

Stay determined for that defines you
The persistence in your heart and
The will of your mind,

Nothing on the surface will define you,
Everything deep in you is what you should find.

Profound

There are many profound things,
They may not all be found in a mound,

Search a little further,
And you will find them.

The Child within the Night

The light finishes its show
And the night steps on stage,
Whether by choice I do not know
Into our sky it comes,
Into space it runs.

What is the night?
It is the twirl of a skirt
in a spirited dance.
It is the graceful tune
of the theater in open air.
It is a playful child,
that leaps across the meadow,
and breaks down the garden fence.

Everyone's Blackboard

Swirling throughout every mind,
Is the magic and wonder of every time,
Of long ago,
Of every snow,
Of every time of human woe,

The magic is flying through your brain,
It comes and goes and leaves a stain,

Close your eyes and you will see black,
Look further and you will see
what your inner self wants you to be,
The beauty of imagination has no fee,

You see black and think the world is shut out,
You open your eyes and start to pout,
"I don't see anything cool."
You may say,
"This is blackness is as worthy as drool."
You may say,
But when you see black the world
just got closer.

Straps!

Straps, straps, straps,
To keep track of them all,
Would take a thousand maps,

There are so many,
And I'll bet more than a penny
That I could lose track of them all.

Oh, why stall?
Because a strap fell off?
Oh!
Well, that is the grade of fifth, fellows!
And soon this will all be a myth,

But for now,

Just keep track of those straps!

Patterns

Patterns are in everything,
Patterns are beautiful,
They can tell you about who you are,
And about the people around you too,

They can make you happy,
And sometimes quite snappy!

They dance amongst the clouds,
And flow down through the rain,
They provide thought in an animal's brain,
They are the heart of entire cities,

And show themselves through their
little people pawns,

They ripple through every lake,
And make no mistake,

Patterns are everywhere.

Calendar Memos

Hard ink on a calendar,
Seeping into other months,
A wonderful day,
That lit up like a sun-born ray,
Fades away with each flip,
Fading away,
yet there is still a memory,

Each time you see the ink that has gone through
you remember,
A wonderful event that had occurred
sometime in September,

Even if the note has disappeared
The ink is still there,

A glorious thing it is,
ink thick on a calendar.

Resilience

A dead forest lies at god's knees,
All because of one summer breeze,
That took a spark at lit the flame,

For miles around there is a hollow blackness,
With shreds of evil bounding of its brow,
So deep it chills the last living soul until it is
cold as ice,

There is only a starless silence now,

It scarred the earth and lift timber to gather,
The song of the trees is now a gloomy silence,
And the face of the moon which so proudly stood brightly,
Is worn with loss and a hard fight,

But over charcoal field,
And broken hearts,
A speck of green claws out of the burned ground,
To make itself a wonderful tree,

The death of a forest is now at ease.

The Magic in Poetry

Poetry is a spirit renewed
just to fit in the ink of your pen,
Even through being squished and squashed
into the words of a pencil,

It does not holler,

The soul and the mind connect,
They join together every time
to make this magical writing come to life,

A different style
Being squished and squashed
And battered and fuzed,

Without this change
poetry's magic is of no use,

The diversity of this change
is what makes poetry
Magic.

Song

The instant rhyme,
Slips fast in every young tune,
It shall never wrinkle up and shrivel like a prune,

Divine is the sound of every single note,
It swirls around you and tightens,
Sewing itself like a coat,

It provides itself as glasses for the old,
That they magically will never need to hold,

It is a fine toy for every child,
And not to anyone's surprise,
This quote is quite popular,
"Music never dies,"

What does this even mean?
It says music will never go away,
Even about Earth's dying days,

Free with golden wings,
To which beat,
every songbird sings,

A pencil scratches out the tune
so kind and gullible,
The soft egg of music hatches,
Free flowing and free to all,
The music spills and doesn't stall,
into a broken glass
that is a heart,
It works its magic and starts
to
start.

The Opposite Mystery

The land opposite of ours,
A mysterious land of course,
And towers defeated
to pull up drowning knowledge
in the glittering deep sea,

It wraps 'round the Earth like a blanket,
and it holds creatures one hundred ways different from our own,

Foamy waves cling to the shores breathing in the dry land,
And the land grasps the ocean, gazing over its endless blueness,

For now and all eternity,
the sea lies where it is meant to be,

Many lives are held by the sea
dangling on silver rods,

Abundant is the life at sea,
but even more its
Mystery.

A Terrible Fight

Why must humans fight?
Is it to show their might?
When peace is not spoken of,
And war rages on,

When one sees rows and rows
Of white marble graves,
Do they realize then,
That war is not the way,

To kill to live,
Or flee to survive,
That is not a valid life,
Never should one face such strife,

When one sees homes on fire,
And weapons in the streets,
Do they realize then
That war is not the key,

When solemn waves of death
Flow like the ocean,
And countless crystal tears
Flow like the sea,

Do they realize then that war is not the key?

The Story of You

A secret pops,
A leash unlocked,
A heart quickens its steady beat,
A reader gasps,
The artifact?
A mass of archeology,
Built high,
as it towers above the land
flying way up into the sky,

Its structure will never perish,
The discoverer can everlastingly cherish
The abundance of
Mysterious,
Muddy,
Adobe bricks,
That build
A book.

A recorder of history young or old
Waits in the office waiting to be told
About heroes and journeys,
and poets of old,
and writers of old,
and athletes of old,

But the best story that is longing to be told
Is the story of you
And what you've been through.

Life

A single speck,
insignificant,
Can hold a beating heart,
yet to grow,

A yearning soul,
to be unleashed,
A creature grabbing
life's free wings,

Majestic eyes
Awake at sleep,
Floating around,
Taking a peep,

Of a world so wide
And now to cry
For life is open
now.

Grandmother

The woman of before, now old of age
Eyes so big,
Lashes so straight,
Pride rising through every vein,
Love just thrashing through all the pain,

Queen of the kids,
Ruler of the mountain,
Bears five kids who simply adore her,

And one small who sees this in her eyes,
looks through time,
and starts to rise.

Grandfather,

A kind man,
Tall and strict,
Traversed many lands
that bow in his presence,

The early bird,
the nature its home,
Holds a heart
similar to my own,

In a tough chest,
wrought of silver and gold,
Is my grandad,
who holds my love
In his hand.

In the Midst of Me

In the midst of me,
there's a hard-packed core,
and through that core is an iron door,

Around the corner,
two wings evolve,
They open and close
And never stop,

They keep me structured and nice,
and elegant like a butterfly,
They provide me with quickness and grace,
For accomplishment in life is a bitter race,

In the midst of me,
There is a complex core
And past that core
Lies so much more.

Mommy

I run into arms
wide with joy
and
warm with love,

I stare into her adoring eyes,
My heart just melts when she cries,

She is my motto, the figure I try to be,
Enjoyably happy and very funny,

She is a person I rely on
and feelings run free
when I am flying
with my Mommy,

Bendable steel, amazingly beautiful,
Generations run wild within her single touch,

I love her,
She loves
me,

We're the perfect little bunch.

Appa

A lovable lion,
King of the kingdom,
Troubles come,
Troubles fought,

He helped me retrieve
Some of what I had lost,
and
Made me feel good,

Always there for me,
And
I'm sure,
The relationship
between us
will always remain pure.

Beware! The Monster Under the Bed

I know he is there, the monster under my bed,

Growling in my bedroom
Wrecking my head
Wearing his dark, evil cape, just like a costume,
Running with weak legs all through the night,
Battling with this darkness is a gruesome fight.

Yet beyond the thick curtains,
And swirling, blue smoke,
There is beauty in this darkness,
Beauty that is unspoken,

Beauty unlike the bright rays of morning,
Or the lazy afternoon,

If you believe in the night,
The night will believe in you too,
This monster now your best pal,
Is always protecting you.

A Starry Something

Little diamonds glisten in the night,

These creatures can be seen
lighting the dark
like candles in a cave,

Reach out your hand
and you can try to touch them,
Sometimes you can see
yet never touch,

These gems everlastingly enchant me,
So far away, but ever so close,

They illustrate the sky,
and set the bait for
Imagination to come in
leaping
across the night.

Apology to You

For what I have done and will do,
I am sorry for,
And what I've said from what I've read
I am sorry for too,

You may think sometimes,
That I am unforgiving, selfish, and rude,
but that is not true,

There is good in me,
I feel that is right,
And I am very sorry
that I had ever
hurt you,

I am dying to know if I will change
Back into the kind person I was not long ago,

I am going through a phase,
and I know you'll understand what I do,

But I know I still owe this apology to you.

The Face of the Moon

In the night sky
Above dreams and all, and all
Inside the hearts of the stars,

The charm of the night, the heart of our space, lies in the sky,
Turning its white face to shine on our world,
Dangling its light rays to entertain its audience,
Tossing its ribbons to decorate the night,
Causing its followers to love its very thought.

Change

I really do not feel the same,
I see I am changing every day,

In height,
In width,
In behavior,

In ways,
you'll see,

But I will cling to myself,
Even if waves of change crash upon me,
I will reach up to my dreams,
Yank them down and bring them with me
along the odd road of life,

I will do these things I've vowed to do,
I will come to an agreement with myself,
Of who I am, and what I will do
I promise myself that I will.

You've Conquered Your Fears!

Raise the sword,
Point in at your fear,
Charge with bold force,
Scream your mighty cry,
Swing your burly arms,
Welcome your leaping courage,
Slay the brawling dragon,

Turn away,

Acknowledge your victory,
Feel your eyes shining,
Hear your allies shouting,
"You've conquered your nemesis!"
Hear the gods bellowing,
"You've conquered the dragon!"
Hear your mind whispering,
"You've conquered your fears!"

The Tide of Poems

With a flood of emotions
A clap and a boom
A wild, shiny poem
Will come twirling to you,

Faster and faster
The words will spin out,
Until your fingers ache
And you crave to shout

At the top of your lungs
The message you have,

You let it flow through your veins
And envelop your brains
As you cooly surf the billowing waves,

The tide of who you are
Gushes here and there
As your beautiful poem
Starts spewing everywhere.

Energy grows,
And stomps all around,
Now nothing can ever
Bring you to frown,

And simply whatever
you long to see
Is right in front of you with a one and two and three!

Such joy fills your heart
And your lips flip to smile
As you look at the poem
that you have sweetly compiled!

Two-Faced

One is angry,
Unforetold,

One is happy,
And quite bold,

One is sugar,
One is sweet,

One is fire,
Ready to beat,

One is jealous,
One is thrilled,

One is angry,
One is fierce,

One is terrible,
One will pierce,

One is joyful,
Never sad,

One is frowning,
Always bad,

One is two-faced,
Kind and cruel,

And for one to be the simple fool,
Of this dreadful, evil and yet cool,
devil monster is as dangerous as can be,

So please,
Do not let this creature skewer you,
Tear you up,
And torture you,

Hold your head up and sing it loud,

"I am perfect I am me, and am all I need to be!"

Snuggles

On a cold winter's night,
When hot cocoa just won't do the trick,
And you shiver with all your might,
To get a bit warmer,

Just grab a little blanket,
And cuddle up with your family,

Now content,
You can continue happily,

On a big boring day,
When anger rides tides of grief,
It will all be okay,
If you let one little hug
Guide you on your way,

When the sun beams like fireworks,
And the trees shake with glee,
A grand high five,
Will make remaining sadness flee,

On any nice event,
When joy fizzes like bubbles,
It is always quite nice,
To engage in a snuggle.

Flowers

Shimmering, like the stars that shine around my heart,
Withering, as the snow pours on Christmas day,
Swarming, like the clouds that float above my head,
Warming, the hands of those that stroke their leaves,

And they're,

Blooming,
Booming,
Blasting,
Color on the fields,

Bringing,
Stringing,
Life upon life,
Itself.

Dazzle

Dazzle,

Be your own star,
Light up the world like the
moon on its wings,

Dazzle,

Ward off your foe,
Succeed in your battles
With your own
Charm,

Dazzle,

You'll never how far you
Can go
Without pushin' yourself
so,

Dazzle,

Ignore that pain,
No more tears
Streamin' down your face,

Cause you will Dazzle,
Be yourself,
Hey,

You'll never know you
If you're someone else
So,

Dazzle,

Be your own luck,
Nourish your mind with
Encouraging thoughts,

Dazzle,

Simply be you
All the time,

Dazzle,

It's not so hard,
Love yourself,
Do not leave your heart charred,

Dazzle,

There aren't any words left so,
Dazzle

All you need to do is,
Dazzle,

So,

Dazzle.

Embrace!

I stare out the window,
To embrace the day,

So what if the forecast,
Is gray clouds and rain,

I leap out the threshold,
To embrace the sky,

Even if the sun is boiling,
And making me fry,

I jump out of my seat,
To embrace the hail,

Those hard chunks of ice
Will not make me fail!

I stand up and smile,
At the fearsome wind,

For a chilling breeze
Can be quite worthwhile,

And while
Baking,
And freezing,
And chilling,
And sneezing,

I try to start in a way,
That will make my life joyful,

As I set off to embrace the day!

Dream Wolf

I see a wolf running in the trees,
Eyes wide with a hunger but not with greed,
She is pursuing an old dream,
That has left her enchanted,

She spins her beautiful howl,
Telling stories of the past,
Her cub running with her wonders why she hunts
the way she does,

Dreams are possible,
Just try to achieve them
With all the power in your muscles,
And smarts in your brain,

Run mother wolf,
Follow your soul,
Howl your melody,
Live your dreams.

H-A-P-P-I-N-E-S-S

It is an odd thing,
A cheerful thing,
A joyous thing,
A special thing,

It is the releasing of worry in a fresh shower of autumn leaves,
It is the swirling of a flowy skirt as it lights up the ballroom,
It is the colorful, vibrant accomplishment that struts boldly in the mind,

It is happiness,
Simple, wonderful happiness,

It is the first laugh of a baby,
The beat of the drums,
It is the joy of something new
yet the honoring of something old,
It is the unlocking of some curious mystery
which was before untold,

Happiness is alive in everyone,

A simple singularity,
that can explode into an entire universe
can joyfully flip an unhappy face into a dazzling smile,

Happiness should be revealed to everyone,
And worn by anyone,
It will make a dry heart pump with joy!

It is an odd thing,
A cheerful thing,
A joyous thing,

H-A-P-P-I-N-E-S-S,
It is a vital and important key to make your life
a special thing,

A lovely thing,
A cheerful thing,
Keep happiness close to your heart
and you can overcome anything,

All your rain will shine down in rainbows,
Because now you know that happiness is an important thing!

Human

The oddest type,
quite interesting indeed,

We could build up a marvelous world,
then quickly break it down,

We could harm our own people,
just because they are different,

Greedy,
Needy,

This is not human,
This is monster,

Raging battles,
Fiery disputes,
Hopeless wars,
Everlasting feuds,

This is not human,
This is monster,

The ones who hold another's hand,
and pull them through the storm,

The ones that emit hope,
and share it with others,

The ones who love,
The ones who care,
The ones who wish,
The ones who dream,

They are human,
We all started as a single cell,
A single clan,
A single tribe,
A single life,

But as we grew to make, manufacture,
we grew apart,

And we let the hunger for power
take control
over our hearts,

Yet we all know,
The ones who create are human,

Take this chance!

We are all equal,
We are all beautiful,

We can all be,
Human

The Things We do not See

Eyes searching the floor,
Ears listening for a tune,
Heart opening for a glimpse,
The things, dear things, lie in the darkness,
In the blackness of the pond
Under the water of the lake
Across the shadow of a forest
Inside the night of your soul.

I Will

The vivid image still lives in my mind,
I was there with my family, so congenial, and so kind,
We sat under the sunset, and all one could see,
Was the everlasting bond in our strong family,

Then it came,
The malevolent force stringing me to my chains,
This package of a dreary life coming on its way,

They took and took, these demented souls,
And traded all that was precious to me,
as if it was nothing more than a straw of hay,

And they worked me to my limit,
And chilled my very bones,
With the eccentric norm that was set for us "slaves",

Run away you see, I did,
Only to be caught like a dog, fleeing its owner,
Chasing me down hard, and caught me in a corner,
And dragged me back, earn a few whippings I did,
They sent me back to work, as I knew they would do,

I wish o' wish I was as invulnerable as they,
And cause a revelation so deep in one's core,
So my masters would not try to own me no more,

To release my sorrow and say day and night,
"Within us people there should be no fight,
To force more people, and cause them plight,
will not show might."
I will make my masters see the light.
I will.

Ode to my Ocean

A crystal sky,
Wide and light,
With white clouds,
Sketched over it,

I look into the vast sea of blue,
Wondering what I would do,
If I could breathe underwater.

A loud crash awakens me,
I see a wave rolling towards me,
It runs and leaps,
Trying to catch me,
A smile and yell, a simple phrase,
"You can never catch me wise, old wave!"
I run away leaving prints in the sand,

I turn around and the wave is much smaller,
Tiny and weak as it rushes past my feet,
A successor roars and tumbles towards me,
But I am much too far out of reach,
It now gently laps my tiny toes,

As I look down, a shell washes up,
Beautiful but broken,
I pick it up and run my hand along the sharp yet smooth edges,
A thought drifts into my mind like a lost feather of a seagull.
Where is the other half of this shell?
Is it sunk at the bottom of the ocean?
Is it on another beach?
Is it drifting in an undertow to a secret place?

I place the shell back on the smooth sand,
I dance freely on this mysterious land,
And suddenly I am part of the place,
The salty air is part of my breath,
And the sky is part of my thoughts,
And the lovely ocean is part of my life.

I turn around and see people on roller coasters,
Having so much fun,
It looks like they are rolling around on rays of the sun,
Other people are chomping down on corn dogs and churros,

I head back to the Boardwalk,
But the waves are calling my name.
I realize that I'm standing on a fine line between nature and machines.
Yin or Yang.
Old or New.
I choose
my ocean.

A Modern Kissed Nature

I hop out of class and sit on a warm bench,
A tall tree branches over me,
The sound of people
Talking,
Sneezing,
Pages rustling,
Feet sliding,
Doors opening,
Doors closing,
Kids screaming,
Leaves fluttering,
Birds chattering,

Rush into my ears.

I leap onto the bench and touch a tree,
It is so cold!
I won't be surprised if I find myself hugging it,
My feet graze the hard ground,
The sun bakes my arm,
But luckily, a breeze swoops by and tousles my hair,

I am in a modern-kissed nature.
I look around,
Everything looks the same,
Except for the plastic flamingo that looks like a cane,
Nature can come in all different sizes,
I realize the outdoors is truly full of surprises.

What Kung Fu Kicks Up

I exhaustedly saunter over to my car,
And melt into the black leather seat
Pretending I'm fine and that I may have had a good time,
Yet the bruises,

       Cuts,

             Scrapes,

                   and,

                       Splinters,

Do not support my point,
They only argue against it,

I gaze around my studio and remember,
The fast-paced fighting I see on TV,
With wise Kung Fu masters powerful and free,
Well, at this point, that person is not me!

I look at the
Silver points of light flashing on the bamboo sticks,
The broadswords that swing close to the user's body,
The dangerously pointed straight swords slicing through their prey,
And finally the regular plain sticks, standing tall as ever,
All of these weapons I must master and use,
All in a short time,
All for a hard benefit,
All through itchy, annoying scrapes and scratches,

As I remain in this pensive state,
I realize the importance of these weapons,
How they serve me to protect me,

And through these
      Cuts,
           Scrapes,
               Splinters,
     Scratches,
         Bruises,
            and Bumps,

And,

                 Belly flops on the green carpet,
                 Dropping my nose into its sweaty fibers,
                 Tripping over my very own feet,
                 Forgetting my white rubbery shoes,
                 Face planting because of a missed move,
                 Rolling,
                 Tumbling
                 Cartwheeling,
                 Jumping,
                 Dodging,
                 Throwing,

                 And missing...

Through all these wonderful pains of kung fu,

I grow.

I kick.

I punch.

I whack,

And eventually, I master.

The Unknown Death

A small ugly larvae,
Squiggling through a stagnant, smelly pond,

When this little worm grows up
It morphs into a small bug,

And the job of so many of these bugs,
Is to bring upon,
A cruel, terrible death.

From an unknown life in a small raindrop,
An old bottle cap,
An oozy, stagnant pond,
The mosquito becomes notorious,
Ominous,
Murderous,

Killing thousands of people who are unknowing,
And exploiting their ignorance,
To infect their lives
And end them,
Their revenge for being unloved by humans,
Is eliminating these fellows,

Carrying
*   Malaria,*
*   West Nile,*
*   Zika,*
They raise their pungent sword,
And slice an unknowing person,

Well, it was only a simple bump.

Yet it turned this person's last day of life
Into a living death,
Then,
Like savages, they drink up his blood,
To simply live,

This tiny beast,
This malignant disease,
To kill to live,
To live to die,
It makes no difference to this body,
This entity,
This capsule,
There is no soul,

They feel no pain,
No regret,
No worry,
No care,
Just thousands of soulless cases,
And following these mosquitos, like a faithful little puppy,
There is only death.

Neto Nut and Neela

Who wouldn't melt at the sight,
Of a fuzzy black kitten brought into the light,

With his big yellow eyes,
And flat, pushed-in nose,
And his very odd cat clean-up pose,

His vibrant personality,
Quite naughty indeed,
Yet still snuggly and lovely,
Definitely one to need,

Who wouldn't fall in love at the beautiful sight,
Of a white, curly-haired dog brought into the light,
With her hazel eyes,
And floppy pink tongue,
She always is ready for a swim
Or a run in the sun,

Yet a rub on the belly is just fine,
With her favorite chew toy
Everlastingly on her mind,

Many people would agree,
That their pets fill their hearts will such a glee,
And help generate more lovely love,
To sustain their lifetime happy and free,

The simple joy of coming home,
And knowing that waiting there
In their own little dome,
Lies their favorite buddies,

Ready to be found,
And be given lots of love,
And more to give around.

Forever

With a booming voice,
He sang his dream,
He spoke his dream.
And signed his dream,

Every single movement that he made,
Every single step that he took,
Was to freedom,

He changed the minds of so many people,
And when no one could stand up,
He did.

His dream was his guide,
And he guided them,

He fought for the rights of not only his race,
But for humanity,
For people,
We are one,
Forever.

Segregation is not the way to make an ordered system,
Love is.
Forever.

And his dream, it flew on lovely wings,
And lit up the sky,
And lit up minds,
And gave them an idea,

To climb aboard and take to the endless freedom above,

This dream was a revelation,
A secret that was released,
A bright idea that would change a world,
Forever.

And when the bullet ran through his body,
it pierced the hearts of many,
And wounded them,

Yet even though many tried to end him,
They never succeeded,
And they never will succeed,

Because even though he is gone,
the dream is still there.
And it will be
Forever.

Golden-Tinged Wings

During the night,
On golden-tinged wings I fly,

During the day,
My soul cries because of the chains digging through my flesh.

Chaining me to this dreadful life
is slavery that tore me out of the sky in the first place,

Every time I try to fly away,
Running, jumping,

to leap away,

Whatever I try,
All my schemes, plots, plans, and maneuvers,
They all die,
At the hand of my master,
My owner,
My supposed leader,

They all grow colder
Towards my dark figure,
And every time I try to spread my wings and fly far, far away,

Every single time,

I miss the eye,
Watching me,
Belonging to my malicious overseer,
And,
I am dragged ruthlessly back to the ground,

My bonds grow stronger,
My luscious wings ever weaker,
Turning wrinkled from abuse,
Becoming crinkled from lack of use,

And the promise of freedom on my golden-tinged wings,
Slowly fades, day by day.

Now there is no scheme,
No way to escape,
No way to leap up and fly far away,

My wings have no power,
My chains with such grip,
So that I am chained to the barn door,
Just glimpsing the outside,

I pray that one day,
I will be let loose,

Yet I can't escape,
Will I ever?

My only dream is to spread my wings,
And escape my master,
To escape this commanding telling me what to do,
To escape this lack of control,
To escape my ragged clothes,
To escape these dirty nights sleeping with pigs,
To escape this world,
Simply this world,

There is one question that is raging in my mind,
Will this world ever change?

Will my people ever be free,
With the right of will,

And the right of speech,

To have educated children just like any other,
To share with other people and be loved by each other,
To have a world filled with peace,

And in which every person flies,
With beautiful golden-tinged wings,

Way up into the sky.

Freedom to be Free

To journey to worlds that you never have known,
Through carefully placed words it was slowly sewn,
Just open the cover and there you go,
Traveling to wherever your eyes desire,

A mystery awaits, begging for you to come and see,
A new friend beckons you and hands you a key,
To walk hand in hand and discover new lands,
New feelings,
New adventures,
New thoughts,

New stories,

From one book you're lead to another,
And from that to another adventure,
And enjoy whatever you want,
Whenever you feel it is time,

Because when you are reading
You have the freedom to be free.

On and on...

Whatever you call it,
The ocean,
The sea,
A great pool of water,
It is calling to me,

A gigantic puddle,
The best friend of trees,
Nothing can change,
The view that one sees,
As they enter the sweet space,
Of vast blue seas,

A sea view of beauty,
Death,
Delight,

A world full of balance,
All day,
All night,

A whole other universe,
Bigger than our own,
That contains thousand of creatures,
Never alone,

I love the deep waves,
As they swirl to the sea,
Calling and begging me,
To go swim free,

I love the creatures talking,

And playing in the sand,
And the shells that traverse,
So many lands,

The waves that crash on the shore,
Are the drum of my heart,
The views are my eyes,
Leading me on,

And the fish are my friends,
Flipping around all day,

On a day with the ocean,
You can never simply lay,
But must peer in every corner,
And feel every water,

For in a world so close,
Yet so far,

There is much to look for.
Swimming on and on...

The Human Trace

For millions of years people have looked to the sky,
It has become an instinct,
many don't know why,

We have traveled great distances far and wide,
To get a glimpse of something from the outside,

Our Earth is too small for modern day standards,
Yet it is not Earth that is small
it is us all,

Every problem that we have,
Every new step that we make,
Seems insignificant when you're way up in space,

Yet through our own civilization,
We have expanded,
Taken our earth and had it branded,
With human success,
Because no matter how tiny we are,
Through every generation we have raised the bar,

Through constant growing years,
from cavemen to CEOs,
Humans have developed,
That is the way our history goes!

But still through our mass civilization,
A part of our hearts wonders about the creation,
that is the big, gaping universe so much larger than our Earth,

The hunger for more knowledge drives deep in human roots,

A sense of enchantment knowing that there is so much more,
could never turn this space into a bore,
For deep down in our hearts we face,
The real truth about the human race,
That when we compare ourselves to the expanding space,
We are nothing but a tiny trace.

On our Earth,
We expand and grow,
Our achievements move quickly to and fro,

So with our tiny little heads,
And puny little bodies,
Let's try and make our wonderful little lives
the best they can be.

ABChildren Destined Eternally
For Giddy Happiness

Children are foolish is so many ways,
Jump off a skateboard,
Or fall off a sleigh,
There are so many ways to act silly,
To spin yourself 'round till you go crazy,
So this poem is for children
Who love to play
Even in a crazy way,

A is for Archie who wore slippery socks,
B is for Bella who jumped off the docks,
C is for Clara who danced her nights away,
D is for Daniel who ate worm decay,
E is for Ernie who wore down his shoes,
F is for Francis who was singing with "MOOO"s
G is for Gerrard who cried out "Wolf!"
Well, he lied!
H is for Hera who got stuck on the slide,
I is for Ivy who was hugging a pole,
J is for Jewels who dug a large hole,
K is for Kitty who brought home a vole!
L is for Louie who stepped on his hand,
M is for Maria who was swimming on land,
N is for Nancie who drank water too fast,
O is for Ollie who took up the mast,
P is for Polly who set fireworks,
Q is for Quinn who hacked the networks,
R is for Roger who was chasing his dog,

S is for Samantha who fell into a bog,
T is for Tania who stayed up too long,
U is for Una who was smacking a gong,
V is for Vera who jumped on her bed
W is for Wanda who ate pencil lead,
X is for Xavier who gambled with dice,
Y is for Yasmin who played with head lice,
And finally,
Z is for Zelda who just wanted to play.

About the Author

Ava Arasan *is a thirteen-year-old author. Ava loves to write poetry and often finds herself doing just that in her spare time. Her poems express her deepest emotions and concerns. She believes that "poems are the reflection of the heart" and wrote this book to share her messages. When Ava is not writing poems, she is reading, singing, practicing the piano, or playing sports. Ava lives in Cupertino, CA with her mother, father, dog, and kitty.*

Printed in the United States
By Bookmasters